God Heard My Cry

JUDY ABEL LUTON

Outskirts Press, Inc.
http://www.outskirtspress.com

ISBN: 978-1-9772-4522-9

Cover Photo © 2021 Allison G. Bullard. All rights reserved - used with permission.

Outskirts Press and the "OP" logo are trademarks belonging to Outskirts Press, Inc.

PRINTED IN THE UNITED STATES OF AMERICA

No truer have those words been, "People come into our lives for a reason", then having met Judy. She is like having sunshine in a cup. She seems to radiate joy and kindness wherever she goes. I haven't always given God the credit for how circumstances and people line up in our lives. Judy is proof that God has a plan. Some are given the toughest of paths in order to prove His love for all of us through their testimony and resilience. When we are weary, we have Him to lean on. I am honored to have my painting used as the cover. Thank you.

Allison Bullard

The Best Friend I Ever Had

I loved my best friend because He first loved me.
How do I know this?
He waits on me each morning to spend time
with Him
He stays close by my side all day long
He guides my every step
He sets an example for me to live by
He restores my faith in Him and others
He shows me that I don't ever need to fear
tomorrow because He is with me today, yes-
terday, and tomorrow
He fills me full of Hope
He loves me just as I am
He lets me rest in Him
He shows me when I am wrong
He is there for me when no one else is
He is preparing a place for me to live with
Him someday
A special place where we can spend eternity
together
-Judy Abel-Luton, 1995

Table of Contents

CHAPTER 1

The Day My Life Changed Forever

In my distress I called upon the Lord,
And cried out to my God;
He heard my voice from His temple,
And my cry came before Him
even to His ears."
Psalm 18:6 (NKJV)

I HAD JUST arrived at the restaurant when the hostess walked over to our table. She asked if there was a person by the name of Judy Abel. I answered, "Yes," and she said there was a phone call at the front desk. I picked up the phone saying, "Hello?" The voice on the other end was my husband, Bob, but I could barely hear him.

In a very hushed voice, Bob said that our son, Craig, was gone.

I asked him to please repeat what he had said. That time I heard him, and I asked, "What do you mean?"

"**Craig is dead**," Bob replied.

My life as I had known it was no longer.

The day was supposed to be a very special day. I was excited because my Mary Kay Senior Sales Director, Gloria Moyer, was visiting from Florida. We were going to dinner with two other Mary Kay Directors, Norma Abrams and Sarah Furnish, as soon as I got off work. And then Bob's phone call came.

I got off the phone and went into the

dining area where my friends were sitting. I told them that I needed to go home. They told me what to do from that point on because I was in shock. My friend, Norma, took my car keys, and she went to get my mother. The rest of us got into Sarah's car. We were all crying all the way to my house. To this day, I do not know what would have happened if God had not been with us.

When we got inside the house, some of our church family were already there. They were trying to comfort my husband, Bob. I ran to him and we both cried and held each other for some time. I sensed God's presence all around us that evening. We were showered with His love and compassion. What a blessing friends are in a situation like this.

A couple from our church who were good friends of ours, told me that they were concerned about Bob. He was not feeling very well at all. They asked me if they could call our doctor to see if he had time to see Bob. The doctor said to bring him in. After an examination, he gave Bob some medicine to help him get some much-needed sleep.

The next morning, our house was full of family, neighbors, and church friends. Bob and I were both still in shock, but we had to start making plans to bury our son. While we were doing that, my Mary Kay friends came to our house to run the sweeper and dust. Another close friend, Janet, came and brought paper goods which were a big help. A friend of mine from Edmond Women's Club, Veta Roberts, called and offered to house sit during the funeral. She was a real blessing to us. It seemed that our house was full of angels helping prepare us for the days ahead. At that time, all that I could think about was that we were burying our son, and I felt that my heart would be broken forever.

The next few days were a blur and were filled with making funeral arrangements. Bob and I were so grateful to have such wonderful family and friends to help us get everything ready for the days ahead. Angie, one of my closest friends, owned a nail shop in Edmond. She closed it for the day of the funeral in honor of Craig and spent the whole day with Bob and I, even riding to the church with us for the funeral service. Angie sat next to me, patting my hand, and comforting me all the way. God was using her to remind me that He was there, loving us the whole time.

When we got to Cathedral of the Hills Assembly of God Church, it was full of people, some we had not seen in a long time. Our Pastor, Ron McCaslin, officiated along with Reverend Jimmy Hodges and Reverend Richard Hogue. Each of these men were an important part of our lives. Most of the service, Bob and I were in a fog. Neither one of us could believe that this was happening. We never imagined that we would be burying one of our children.

As we began to realize what God was doing in our lives, the scripture in Romans 8:28 came to mind, "And we know that all things work together for good to those who love God, to those who are called according to His purpose". (NKJV) Later Bob and I were told that people we knew, who had quit going to church for various reasons, had decided to come back to the faith after the funeral. Knowing that friends had found their way back to God was a blessing to both of us. In our sadness, God had brought joy to us and to others. Our Heavenly Father loves His children more than we could possibly know.

We knew that Craig had been living with his girlfriend at her house, and they had just had a fight. We never found out the details of the fight. Craig had gone out to his pick-up, gotten his gun, and returned to the house where he shot himself in front of her. I want her to know if she is ever reading this book, that we do not hold her responsible in any way.

Three weeks after Craig died, I returned to work. I loved my job and the people that worked with me. The hardest part was when someone would ask, "How are you doing?" Sometimes I could not hold back the tears, which made it difficult for those who were trying to comfort me. However, I had several good girlfriends who I could pour my heart out to, and they would just listen. I could also talk to my Savior at any time. Jesus was right there with me. He was my stronghold every day. I knew that He loved us and wanted us to stay close to Him. As Matthew 28:20 says, "And surely I am with you always, to the very end of the age." (NIV)

After a while, we got back to some sort of normal. My husband and I took it one day at a time. We each dealt with the loss of Craig differently. For example, he went back to work soon after the funeral and kept busy with tax extensions that he had to finish. After work, he would come home and change clothes and either go out to the barn to work on a project or get on the mower to tend to our five acres. He would wait until I got home from work for me to prepare dinner. Then, he would come in to eat dinner with me and go back outside until it was dark. When he came in, he would go straight to bed. That was his routine for quite some time.

Since I was alone a lot of evenings, my thoughts would turn back to our life before Craig's death. I wondered, "What did we do wrong?" We loved our children and tried to teach them good values. Did we miss something along the way? I know the devil wants us to blame each other or ourselves in these situations. Neither of us wanted to do that.

Craig had come over to our house on the Saturday before he died on Tuesday. He and I had a good talk, and he visited with his dad that day as well. Nothing seemed wrong with him at all. When Bob and I were finally able to discuss our feelings about Craig, one of the first discussions we had was, "What happened and why didn't we see the signs that something was bothering him?" Be careful not to start the blame game because nobody ever wins in that.

We had been told that when parents lose a child (in our case, a 26 year old young adult) one of two things eventually happen: the parents end up in a divorce, or they hold tight to each other and the Lord. Fortunately, my husband Bob and I had a good relationship with Jesus our Lord. We both knew that Jesus was right there with us. We believed His promise that, "He would never leave us," and He never has.

I finally realize why it has taken me so long to get started writing this book. It is because I am having to relive this part of my life. While I was still home one day, I asked myself, "What would Craig want me to do?" I knew that Craig would tell me, "Mother, ahead of you is a fork in the road. One path is muddy. If you go that direction, you will either lie down and wallow in it and take everyone who loves you down that path with you. The other path, you see Jesus. And you let Jesus take you by the hand and lead you the rest of the way home."

CHAPTER 2

Our Son, Craig

"Yea, though I walk through the valley of
the shadow of death, I will fear no evil; For
You are with me; Your rod and Your staff,
they comfort me."
Psalm 23:4 (NKJV)

OUR SON, CRAIG Allen, was born on May 11th, 1964 in Oklahoma City, Oklahoma. Craig was easy to care for as a baby. When I had errands to run, I could put him in the stroller, and he would go right to sleep. That changed when he was old enough to crawl out of the stroller. He would hide from me under the clothing racks at the stores! After a while, I knew where to look for him and would remind him that he had to stay close to his mother, or he would be in deep trouble when we got home. He did not like to be punished, so most of the time, he would remember not to misbehave again.

Craig's personality was similar to mine. We both loved people, enjoyed playing games, and just wanted to be a part of whatever was going on in general. The only problem we encountered with Craig was that in his teenage years, he was more of a follower, so we needed to know who the leader in the group was, and where they were leading the others. This meant that his father and I always made it a point to get to know his friends and their parents.

Craig could also be a hothead sometimes. When this happened, his father would sit him down and talk to him about his temper. Bob told him about how he had a problem with his temper when he was younger and had to learn how to control it.

One of the funniest times with Craig was when he was 15 years old. He was a big fan of Evel Knievel. When we moved to our house in the country, Bob bought him a dirt bike and told him that he could only ride it on our acreage, never on the street. Craig and his close friend, Troy, were riding in our back pasture, and they had built a ramp to ride the dirt bike off. I told both boys to be very careful and to not be too wild.

Craig and Troy had been outside for more than an hour when I happened to notice Craig lying on the sofa in the den. I asked him why he was not outside riding the dirt bike anymore. He said that he was just resting. I raised my eyebrow, looking at him, and said, "Did you get hurt?" He sheepishly admitted that yes, he and Troy had been trying to jump like Evel Knievel, and Craig had landed in a bad place for boys to land. I think Craig learned a good lesson from that one!

Craig was a sweet, loving person. When he was older, Craig and I had fun doing different things together. One New Year's Eve, Bob and I had plans to go out with some friends of ours to Bricktown's New Year's Eve celebration in Oklahoma City. Bob ended up not feeling well, so Craig offered to go with me. Craig knew most of our friends, so they wanted Craig to go with us. We ended up having one of the television stations interview us. When we told them that I was his mother, they did not believe us. We had such a good time, and I will always remember my night out with my son.

I miss Craig so much, but I'm comforted to know that he is with Jesus now.

CHAPTER 3

A Girl Named Judy

In their hearts humans plan their course,
but the Lord establishes their steps.
Proverbs 16:9 (NIV)

MY NAME IS Judy Luton, and I was born in Enid, Oklahoma. My family and I moved to Oklahoma City when I was six months old. My father, Roy Grimes, traveled for a living and my mother, Alta, was a stay-at-home mother. My mother and I were home alone during the week, and usually, my father came home on Thursday night. He was at home with us on the weekends. My parents were not churchgoers, so my neighbors who attended church would ask me to go with them.

As a young child, I was curious about God and wanted to know more. Thanks to my neighbors, I was able to visit many different churches. When I was 12 years old, my mother said that I could join a church of my choice, so I decided to join the Linwood Methodist Church where my friends attended.

One of my friends who attended Linwood Methodist asked me to go to church camp with her that summer. Thankfully, my mother agreed to let me go. I was so excited to be able to learn more about God that summer.

One night, we had a youth service. They took us up on a hill close to camp where I saw a wooden cross. The pastor explained to us how Jesus had died on that cross for our sins. He told us that we could ask Jesus into our hearts personally. I prayed that night and asked Jesus to accept me as His child. After that evening, I was so excited to tell my family and friends about Jesus and what had happened to me.

When I returned home, I immediately told my parents about the decision I had made.

Early on I knew that God had something special for me to do. I started to spend more time at church learning about Him. One of the things that I did was volunteer at the church to help whenever they needed me. I became involved with Methodist Youth Fellowship (MYF). I think that was the beginning of God teaching me to trust Him and have faith that He would guide my steps throughout my life.

My first experience with grief was when I was 14 years old, my grandfather died. I remember so well what happened because it was extremely hard on me. I loved my grandfather very much, and when I was little, I spent a great deal of time with him on my grandparents' farm.

The day he died; I was at school. My mother called the school to ask my teacher if I could be excused from class that day. I had no idea what was going on until I got home. When she told me, I started to cry and could not stop for quite some time. It seemed like it was not real.

A few days later, we went to the funeral and I fell apart, big time! Maybe it was my age, but it hit me hard. Before that time, I had not really thought about anyone dying. My parents did not talk about death before then, so it was hard for me to understand.

When I was a senior in high school, we had our prom night at a country club in Oklahoma City. One of the couples that I knew well had a wreck when they were leaving the dance, and the girl was killed. She was a very popular girl, and everyone was in shock. That was also awfully hard for me to accept.

After that, I was scared to talk about death and grief. Even when I was an adult, my mother would start to tell me what to do when she died, and I would change the subject or just not listen.

Even with these experiences with death, I had no idea what the impact of the loss of loved ones was going to have on my life. I am grateful that I already knew Jesus before losing my grandfather because I would need Him then, and I would need Jesus even more for what was ahead of me.

CHAPTER 4

Life is Good!

"Every good gift and every perfect gift
is from above, and comes down from the
Father of lights, with whom there is no vari-
ation or shadow of turning."
James 1:17 (NKJV)

DURING MY JUNIOR year of high school, I met a boy that would later become my husband, Bob Abel. He went to John Marshall High School. He was also a Methodist, so we began visiting each other's churches on Sunday night. It was important to me that I stay active in my MYF youth group, so that is why we took turns. After Bob graduated from John Marshall, he enrolled at Oklahoma State University. I was a senior at Northwest Classen High School. Bob was a freshman at Oklahoma State University in Stillwater, Oklahoma.

It was hard for both of us to be apart, so I decided that since it was my Senior year, I would get involved in school activities such as Student Council, Coronet Pep Club, and helped on the program cover for the senior class play we were doing.

After graduating from Northwest Classen, I decided to enroll at OSU for the fall classes. Bob and I were able to spend more time together, so we talked about our future plans. We talked about getting married and having a family. When the school year was over, we went to talk to our parents about getting married. Neither of our parents were happy because they wanted us to graduate first. Now that I am older, I look back on this and understand their concerns, but we were persistent, and both sets of parents finally gave in.

We were married on September 2nd, 1960. I was able to get a job working at the telephone company in Oklahoma City. Bob also got a job at the telephone company where he worked the day shift and took night classes at the University of Central Oklahoma in Edmond. We both liked our jobs, and we worked with some nice people.

Like most young couples, we had planned on waiting to have our family after we both graduated from college, but God had another plan for us. Our first child was born the following year on August 29th, 1961 and we named her Tamara.

When she was born, Bob wanted me to stay home, so I quit my job to be a full-time mother. It was difficult for Bob to work eight hours a day and then go to school at night, but he wanted to finish college so that he could take care of his family.

Bob graduated from Oklahoma City University on May 15th, 1964, and he was on the Dean's Honor Roll. Our second child, a son, Craig Allen, was born on May 11th, 1964 just in time to be Bob's graduation present.

We had a good life and things seemed to be going well. We stayed involved at Linwood Methodist Church for several years, but it was getting difficult to drive that far every Sunday to attend the services, especially with two small children to get ready. About that time, there was a new Methodist church being built right across the street from our house. The youth pastor came over several times to invite us to come visit, so we decided one Sunday morning that we would go check it out. The church was just starting to grow. After we had attended there for a while, the pastor asked us to help with a newlywed class. We loved getting to know the young people in the class. To this day, we are still friends with quite a few of them.

I am grateful, daily, for the things that have happened in my life that have drawn me closer to Jesus. He has always been there, even when I did not know who he was. He has always been right beside me, directing my steps and placing people in my life for me to love and be loved by.

CHAPTER 5

Moving to the Country

"Therefore, if anyone is in Christ, he is a new
creation; old things have passed away; behold
all things have become new."
2 Corinthians 5:17 (NKJV)

ONE EVENING, AFTER tax time was over, Bob came home and asked me to sit down with him to talk. As I sat down, he said that he had been thinking about moving to a place where we could have some space for our children to have animals. Our daughter had always wanted a horse, and our son wanted a dirt bike to ride. I was surprised that Bob had even seriously considered it. He told me that he had made an appointment for the next day to go look at acreages and that a friend from his fraternity was going to come pick us up. He wanted to show us a property in Edmond first. It was just off Route 66 and east of the interstate.

When we drove in, I immediately fell in love. We had not even gone inside yet. This house was perfect for us, but it was a problem that it was in Oklahoma City's school district. Our realtor was certain that we could get that changed. He took us out to a couple more properties in Yukon and in Mustang, but we did not find anything there that we liked. The property in Edmond still had our attention.

Over the next few days, the house in

Edmond was all that I could think about. Even when I went to bed, I would dream about that house and I am sure that Bob was thinking about it too. We decided to go back out there to look at it again, and I decided to check with the Edmond School Board to see if we could get them to let our children enroll in their district instead of Oklahoma City. They told me that we would have to live in the house before they would even talk to us about it. I should have known that was not a good sign. Eventually, we decided to buy the Edmond house and we moved in the month of August in 1975.

At that time, our children were teenagers. They were so excited about this move to the country. It was a big change for us. Most of our family and friends thought we were crazy, but we were so happy. The day we moved from our house in Oklahoma City to Edmond, a close friend of ours, Janet, came over early that morning to help me load up my car and her car. Then, we headed to Edmond and our new home.

What a day that was! We made three trips

back and forth. Bob had to work that day, so we hired a moving van to take the larger items to Edmond for us. When Bob came home from work, everything was at the new house. At the time, Bob was working in downtown Oklahoma City for an accounting firm, and he did not like the long drive. After we got settled in our new house, he made his office in the front living area. It turned out to be perfect for his clients to come in our front door to his office.

The situation with the Edmond School Board did not work out in the way that we had hoped. After several attempts to get them to change their mind, we enrolled our daughter, Tamara, in John Marshall High School, and our son, Craig, in Hoover Middle School, both in Oklahoma City School District.

After we got settled into our new life in Edmond, we began to look for a new church home. At the time, our children were teenagers and were a little hard to please about going to church anywhere at all. But since we were the parents, we had the final say about where we would go.

Janet, our friend that had helped us move, and her family moved to Edmond right after we did. Our families had both attended the same church for several years in Bethany. After some difficulty finding a new church home, Janet called to see if we would like to visit a new church that was having a revival close to where we lived. I told her, yes, we would plan to go with them the next Sunday.

Janet called us that Sunday morning to tell us that her family was sick so they would try again the next weekend. I was so disappointed. I tried to get Bob and the kids out of bed and dressed so that we could go, but they would not budge. I decided to get dressed and just go by myself.

I was not yet familiar with Edmond, so I stopped at a grocery store where a lady was walking out just as I pulled up to the curb. I got out of my car and walked up to her, introduced myself, and told her my situation. I told her that I had heard there was a church meeting in the cafeteria at Memorial High School, and could she please tell me how to get there? She gave me directions to the school. I thanked her and left.

When I found the school I went inside, and an usher came to welcome me. I looked up to see an old friend that my husband and I had played bridge with in Oklahoma City. He said that he thought that I would love the church, then seated me near the front. The service had already started so I listened as the pastor shared from God's Holy Word, and I began to cry.

At that point in my life, I needed God more than ever. My father was in the hospital, dying, and my teenagers were driving me crazy. I needed my Savior desperately. After church, I called Bob and asked him to meet me for lunch so that we could talk about what I had just experienced.

We ate lunch and talked about what was going on in our lives. I told him that I needed the Lord's guidance and asked him to consider going to church with me that evening. He said that he would, so we went back that evening. I knew that I had made the right choice. We started to attend every Sunday, getting to know people and make friends that would be friends for the rest of our lives.

One evening after dinner, when we had been attending the church for a while, the doorbell rang. When I opened the door, I was surprised to see Pastor Hogue and another man from the church standing there. My first thought was, "Oh no. Bob is going to think that I asked them to come talk to him." Not so. I was as surprised as he was. I invited both men to come inside.

At first, they told us about the church and how it had been started. We told them how we had come to Edmond and loved the community and enjoyed the church services. Pastor Hogue then asked if we had attended a church in Bethany, and we told him about the church in the Bethany area that we had attended for several years. Then, he asked us if we had a personal relationship with Jesus.

Bob and I looked at each other for a few seconds. I replied, "yes," and Bob replied that he just was not sure. Pastor Hogue asked Bob how long we had been married and if he loved me more now than when we first got married.

Bob said, "Of course." Pastor explained that each day we know Jesus personally, we would learn to love Him more and more. That following Sunday at the close of the service when they had an altar call, Bob took my hand and we both went together to commit our lives to Jesus.

Thank goodness for that move to the country.

CHAPTER 6

God Knew What We Needed

"Through the Lord's mercies we are not
consumed, because His compassions fail
not. They are new every morning;
great is Your faithfulness."
Lamentations 3:22-23 (NKJV)

IT HAD BEEN two years since Craig's death, and Bob and I were taking each day as it came. Some days were good, and others were not, but we knew we were not alone.

One afternoon, I was at the front desk at my job, answering the phones. As I picked up the phone, I heard my husband's voice on the other end. We chatted for a few minutes, then Bob tells me that he had gotten a call from his doctor's office. The doctor told him that he had experienced several "silent heart attacks." I sat there, not responding for a few seconds thinking, "What in the world is a silent heart attack?" He said that the doctor told him that a person who had a silent heart attack may have had no warning signs at all. He wanted Bob to come into the office so that they could do some tests to see what was going on.

My mind was racing, thinking, "Here we go again. Lord help us." The tests confirmed that Bob had definitely had two or three silent heart attacks in the past. It could have been when Craig passed, but we were not sure. The result showed that Bob needed bypass surgery. The Labor Day holiday was coming up, so the doctor that was doing the surgery was going to be out of town. He wanted to wait until he returned from his vacation to do a triple bypass on Bob.

Our 33rd wedding anniversary was that weekend. I asked God to help Bob make it through the surgery, because I could not continue without him. Some of my friends at the office found out that it was our anniversary, so they had a lovely dinner sent to our house since we were not able to go out to dinner because of Bob's condition. We had such a wonderful time. I even put a candle on the table to make the evening special for us. God puts certain people in our lives just at the right time.

Thankfully, the surgery was successful, and Bob was back at work within three weeks. He said that he felt better than he had in a long time.

That experience taught us to trust Jesus instead of ourselves. We were slow learners, but God had gotten our attention. We both knew that He knew what was best for His children.

God had been with us each step of our journey. He was preparing us for the next steps in that journey.

Shortly after, we began attending Cathedral of the Hills Assembly of God Church (now called Spring Creek Assembly of God). We were asked to be sponsors in the high school class with some other couples. We agreed to help wherever they needed us because we loved working with the young people so much.

Later, our pastor announced that the church was going to start a College and Career Class. They were asking volunteers to help lead it, and I turned to Bob and asked him if we could help. He knew that I loved the college-age students, and he said that we could try and see how it worked out. A couple who were friends of ours were the lead sponsors, and we were the assistants. At first, we only had one girl coming, but the five of us would get down on our knees and pray for almost an hour, then fellowship with each other before we went home.

Gradually, more people began to come, and the group was beginning to grow. Thank the Lord! The class grew until we averaged between 45 to 50 in attendance. We helped teach Sunday school, and since we lived on five acres, most of the class parties were at our house. During the next few years, the students were a big part of our lives. The relationships with them were strong, and we needed it as much as they did, if not more.

Quite often, the phone would ring and the voice on the other end would be a student asking if they could drop by to talk about something that was bothering them. No matter how busy we were, we would say to come on over. I believe that God put those young people in our lives at just the right time.

CHAPTER 7

Our Daughter, Tamara

"I have no greater joy than to hear that
my children walk in truth."
3 John 1:4 (NKJV)

OUR DAUGHTER, TAMARA Lynn, was born on August 29th, 1961. She had the prettiest red hair. I know all parents and grandparents say that their baby is beautiful, and that is exactly what we said about Tamara.

As I said previously, Bob and I decided that it would be a good idea for me to quit my job so that I could be a stay-at-home mother. I am so glad that I was able to do that. Tamara and I had so much fun together, and I loved being her mother.

When Tamara was a baby, I would spend a lot of time trying to get her to talk. When she finally said her first words, Bob and I were so excited to hear her say, "Dada." It was sweet music to our ears. We could hardly wait for her to really start talking. When that happened, we quickly realized that she would be talking all the time!

From the time Tamara was small, we knew that she had a strong will. She was not easily intimidated by others, and she was a natural-born leader rather than a follower. Sometimes that was a good thing and other times not so much. We had to watch who her friends were and get to know their parents. Like most parents, we wanted her to have friends that would encourage her in the right way.

After we moved to Edmond and she started at John Marshall High School, her father and I thought it would be a good time to get her a horse. Tamara had talked about wanting to learn how to ride for some time. We bought her a registered Paint and Quarter horse named Sunshine. She was a beautiful horse, and Tamara fell in love with her immediately.

Bob and I thought that it would be wise for Tamara to have riding lessons, so we looked for a good teacher. We found a young lady that had been training horses for several years. She was willing to take our daughter as a student. It was not long before Tamara was ready to compete in horse shows. She loved barrel racing and was good enough to win some ribbons. It was a lot of fun for our entire family.

As time went on and Tamara was getting older, she became interested in boys and not so much in her horse. Her dad told her that she had to make a choice between the horse and the boys. She decided that dating would be more fun. Well, a few years later, she told her dad and I that she had made a mistake, giving up her horse for boys. Sunshine would have been the better choice!

Tamara was like her father in that they both were very disciplined. When she had a project to do, she kept at it until she was finished. After she graduated from high school, she decided to enroll at Oklahoma State University. Tamara only went one year to OSU. She decided to find a job and found one with a large oil company in Oklahoma City. She went to work in the accounting department and worked there for several years.

When she first came back home from Stillwater, her Grandma Grimes, my mother, wanted her to move in with her so Tamara did. Tamara and her grandma were very close, so it worked out well for the both of them. Later, one of Tamara's best friends, Marion, was looking for a place to live, so Tamara and Marion found a small house for rent. Marion became like family to all of us.

Around that time in her life, Tamara met

a young man named Mark Hendrix. They started dating and became serious after a few months. Mark asked Bob if he could marry Tamara. Bob happily said yes. We all liked Mark, so we were excited about the wedding, especially Tamara's grandma. Their wedding was at St. Luke's Methodist Church, and it was absolutely beautiful.

Tamara and Mark both had good jobs, so they were busy during the week. When we could get together, we would have dinner then play either card games or board games. Those times are wonderful memories for me as I look back on my life.

I will never forget the day that Tamara called me and said, "Mother, are you sitting down?" I said yes, and she proceeded to tell me that she and Mark were going to have a baby. I almost fell out of my chair and started yelling for Bob to come hear what Tamara had just told me. He grabbed the phone and told his daughter congratulations. What an exciting day that was.

Mark and Tamara had been married almost ten years, so this was quite a surprise. They had said that they were not planning on having any children but had changed their minds. We were sure glad they did because we wanted to be grandparents. Lexi Shea Hendrix was born on November 28th, 1994.

CHAPTER 8

"Lord, What Else Can Happen?"

"The Lord is near to those who
have a broken heart, and saves such as
have a contrite spirit."
Psalm 34:18 (NKJV)

ON JANUARY 4ᵀᴴ, 2004, we had a house full of college students watching the Oklahoma University football game on our television. Our phone rang, and I answered it. My son-in-law, Mark, was on the other end telling me that something was the matter with Tamara. Mark had called for EMSA to take her to the hospital. At the time, he had no idea what was wrong with Tamara, but said he would call us as soon as they arrived at the hospital.

When I hung up the phone, I turned around to tell Bob what Mark had said. The students heard me and asked if they could pray for us. Of course, we said yes. We all held hands as they prayed a beautiful prayer over us. Thank God for prayer warriors! In just a few minutes, the phone rang again. Mark was on the other end telling us to come as quickly as we could. One of the boys got our car keys and took us to the hospital. The rest of the students got into their cars and followed us.

The next thing I remember is the doctors saying that Tamara had an aneurysm, and that she was in a coma. We were all in shock. My thoughts at that point were, "Lord, what else can happen?"

As we looked around the waiting room, it was full of our church family and close friends praying for Tamara and for us. The nurses and doctors were shocked by all of the students that were there with us at the hospital. Those precious students stayed with us all evening and some even until one in the morning. Thank God that we felt His arms wrapping us in His love.

Tamara passed away at six o'clock the next morning. She never regained consciousness. Poor Mark had to go tell his daughter, Lexi, that her mother was gone. Even now as I write this, I think about Mark and Lexi without Tamara.

When Tamara died, she had three children: her stepsons, Dustin and Donald, and her daughter, Lexi, who was nine-years old at the time. Today, Lexi is 26 years old and a beautiful young woman. We are all so proud of her. I know that her mother is proud of her too.

Bob and I struggled for a long time with the fact that we did not get to talk with Tamara before she died. Our hearts were absolutely broken. Knowing that we had not been able to communicate with her before she took her last breath was difficult. As we left the hospital, I said to Bob that I knew God would get us through this time in our lives. Bob looked at me and nodded his head to agree that he believed that also. We both knew that God would take care of us and get us through this most difficult time. Tamara's funeral was packed with our family and friends that were there to help us, just as they had been with Craig.

Now, we had lost both of our children, BUT we had not lost our faith in God. He is still with us and will never leave our side. In the years since that time, I have had many people ask if we ever blamed God for Tamara's and Craig's deaths? My answer has always been an emphatic NO, because we knew that God loved them more than we could ever love them, and He continued to care for us daily.

CHAPTER 9

Job's Trials and Judy's Story

"And the Lord restored Job's losses
when he prayed for his friends.
Indeed the Lord gave Job
twice as much as he had before."
Job 42:10 (NKJV)

AFTER TAMARA DIED, I started thinking about similarities between the life of Job and mine. Bob and I were sitting in the waiting room at OU Medical Hospital talking with our pastor, Ron McCaslin, about what had just happened to our daughter. As we were talking, I told Pastor that even though I had read the story of Job many times, I had never understood how Job must have felt until right now. I know God's Word promises that He will not give us more than we can handle, but I was not sure that I could handle this.

Pastor said that God knew me, and God knew that I would give Him all the glory. I have done my best to follow through with doing what God has asked me to do. Without my faith in the Lord, I would never have made it through the loss of my two children.

I want to make sure that my readers understand that I am not in any way trying to compare my life with Job's life. Job lost everything except his faith in God. I lost the most important people in my life here on earth, and I thank God that my faith grew stronger because of what I had learned.

Recently I was listening to a CD of Max Lucado's titled "For These Tough Times." I had just started to listen when he starts to talk about Job and all the horrible things that happened to him. Mr. Lucado was telling what a good and righteous man Job was, but he only had one shortcoming—he talked too much. I started to laugh because that is something that Job and I have in common.

Satan went to God to ask His permission to attack Job believing that Job would give up on trusting God. God told Satan that he could try, but that he was not allowed to kill Job. When I listened to this story, I thought, "Why did God allow these things to happen to Job and to me?" My story is like Job's in that God was preparing us for the battle with Satan in the days ahead.

At the time when I was going through these horrible things, it seemed unreal to me. As I look back on my journey with God, He was showing me how to trust Him in all situations. All the time with Him, my faith was getting stronger every day. What do you do when your world is crumbling around you? You feel like things will never be the same again. God will show you how He can restore your life with purpose and hope for the future.

One of the best lessons that I learned is that Satan has no power over us. If we focus on God and hold tightly to His hand, Satan cannot defeat us. We, as God's children, are covered by the blood of Jesus. I can attest to God's promise that He will never leave us nor forsake us. When we ask Him into our heart, it is for eternity.

Recently I read Job again to remind myself

of all that Job went through. My favorite part is Job 42:11. It tells how God blessed Job. God restored Job's losses as Job prayed for his friends as God had commanded him to do. God gave Job twice as much as he had before. What an awesome Lord we serve.

I want to give you some scripture to refer to when you are struggling with questions. What can people do when everything is falling apart around them? Where is God in all of this? Is God really in control? Read Isaiah 55:8 and 9. Do you believe God really loves you? If God is for us who can be against us? Read Romans 8:35. Can anything separate us from God? Read Matthew 6:13.

CHAPTER 10

"Oh No, Here We Go Again"

"Let us hold fast to the confession
of our hope without wavering,
for He who promised is faithful."
Hebrews 10:23 (NKJV)

I WISH I could say losing my daughter, Tamara, was the end of my grief story, but sadly it is not. Six weeks to the day after Tamara's death, February 25th, 2004, my husband had a massive stroke.

Bob and I had breakfast together at home, and he left for work early like he always did. About 30 minutes later, our phone rang at home. I answered it, and it was Dan, a friend of ours from church. He was at Bob's office, and he told me that something was the matter with Bob. I asked him what he meant, and he said that Bob had laid down on his desk. I told him to call 9-1-1 and I would be right there.

At this time, we had a student, Kayoko Kamata, from Japan living with us while she was attending the University of Central Oklahoma. I woke her up and told her that Bob was ill. They were taking him to the hospital. She and I both got dressed and were about to leave when the phone rang again. It was Mike Stevenson, who shared office space with Bob. He told me that EMSA said Bob had a stroke and it was an emergency.

They had to get him to the hospital as soon as possible. We drove right to ER at Mercy.

When I arrived at the hospital, the doctors told me that Bob had a stroke and that they needed to perform surgery immediately. Pastor Ron McCaslin and a group of our friends were already at the hospital when Kayoko and I arrived. The doctors needed my permission to operate on Bob, so Pastor and the other friends suggested we pray. They took my hands, and prayed. I knew that I wanted the doctors to do everything that they could for Bob. I was in a fog when this first happened, but the Lord was holding on to me.

Bob survived the surgery but was in critical condition. He was admitted to the ICU for a week, and then moved to a room on the rehab floor. He was in the hospital for three months. One day, I received a call from our "adopted" daughter, Anita Harris, who was the secretary at our church. She called me to tell me that a couple from our church had left an envelope at the church for me. She came up to the hospital and handed it to me. I opened it and there was a card and a check for $1,000. I started to cry and thank God for His faithfulness to us. God always sent us just what we needed when we needed it. There were many miracles along the way, and I appreciated all of them.

While Bob was in the hospital, I was there every day and most nights. This was an extremely stressful time, and I do not think that anybody rests well in the hospital.

One day, one of our good friends from church called and told me that the men in our Sunday School class had all signed up to take shifts staying overnight at the hospital with Bob. Each night, one of them would come and make sure that I got to my car safely. They would stay all night with my husband, so that I could go home and get some rest in my own bed. What a blessing to have friends that cared for us so deeply.

During that time, we had two pugs, Kay-Kay and Piglet. Kay-Kay was my dog, but Piglet was Bob's dog and with Bob being in the hospital for so long, they were missing each other. To remedy this, Greg Morgan, our "adopted" son, rode with me to the hospital.

They stayed in the car while I went to get Bob to bring him down to the outside entrance where the hospital allowed dogs. I got Bob into his wheelchair and took him down to see Piglet. What a reunion! Piglet immediately got into Bob's lap and licked his face from ear to ear. Bob was so excited to see Piglet.

Bob Abel in Mercy Hospital
with the Bunn family.
Charlie, Dona, Brielle and Ethan.

A few days before Mother's Day that year, our other "adopted" son, Charlie Bunn, called me up and told me that he was going to take me to church for Mother's Day. He showed up that morning holding a corsage for me to wear. When we arrived at church, some of the college students were there waiting for us so that we could sit together for the service.

After church, Charlie and his family, Dona, Brielle, and Ethan, took me out to lunch so that we could eat as a family. Then, we went up to the hospital to spend time with Bob. Brielle and Ethan were much younger at the time and sat on Bob's lap in the wheelchair while he took turns letting them ride up and down the hospital hallway. We were all laughing, and it was such a happy moment in a stressful situation. That Mother's Day was extra special to me, and I will remember it forever. It felt nice to have my adopted family always keep me in the loop. The littlest things always meant the most during that time.

On May 15th, I was able to take Bob home. Soon after that, the doctors sent three therapists in to help him recover from the stroke because he could not speak, read, or do much on his own. One of the therapists, Teri, became a very good friend to both Bob and me. She was Bob's favorite, and when he was down, she could make him laugh. During the time she was working with Bob, we got to know her and knew that she was a strong Christian.

I stayed home with Bob for the first year and took care of him. After that year, I needed to get a job to help provide an income. That income would happen as a God thing too.

One day, Bob had a doctor's appointment. He had received a good report from his doctor, so I told him we should celebrate by going to lunch at Panera across from the hospital. As we were eating lunch, I saw a friend from my childhood. When we were getting ready to leave the restaurant, we went over to their table to say hello. Judy and her husband, Dave, looked up and recognized us. Since Judy and I had not seen each other in some time, she was not aware that Bob had a stroke. She asked me how we were doing, and I told her that I was going to be looking for a job.

The first thing she said to me was, "Why don't you come work with me at the wedding chapel?" Judy co-owned and operated a wedding chapel in Oklahoma City called Walnut Creek Wedding Chapel.

I said that I knew nothing about weddings.

Judy said, "I can train you. Just follow me, and I will show you."

I eventually agreed to the job, and what a blessing it and Judy were to me. They made my schedule flexible with Bob's various doctors' appointments and allowed me to be off on Sundays so that I could go to church. The Lord was constantly providing for us in big ways.

One of the first outings that I had with Bob after he came home from the hospital was to get lunch at McLaren's Pantry. I called our friend, Tim Parry, who was one of our college students from our church. I asked him if he had some time to come help get Bob, who was in a wheelchair then, into our car. Tim said of course that he would be glad to help me. The three of us had lunch together and had a wonderful time.

Four years and one day after the stroke, February 26th, 2008, Bob Abel went home to be with Jesus. After four long years of pain and physical limitations, he was finally free. I just imagine that he ran into Jesus' arms when he arrived in Heaven.

There is someone who is a very important part of this story that I want to include. The day that Bob had the stroke at his office, the Edmond Fire Department responded. On the call was a young fireman by the name of Greg Westermire. As Greg was preparing Bob for transport, he took a closer look at Bob. Greg asked Mike Stevenson what Bob's name was. Mike told him that it was Bob Abel.

Greg said, "I know him and his wife. They attended the same church that I did when I was a teenager."

Fast forward, the next time he was in our lives is the day that my husband Bob passed away. See how God works in our lives! Greg was on call at the station when I called 9-1-1. When they got to our house, he stayed up in the kitchen talking with me while the others were downstairs with Bob. He was so nice to me, and I needed a friend at the time.

There is more to the story. That evening, I had a lot of family, church friends, and neighbors that had come by to let me know they cared. When the doorbell rang, I went to open the door and standing there were two firemen holding a cake. One of them was Greg Westermire, and the other was Chad Weaver. I asked them to come in.

When they came into the kitchen, everyone saw the cake that they had made for us. Some of the men started to joke with them about making cakes in their spare time, and we all started to laugh. It was just what I needed, and it was a blessing to all of my company. Thank God for men like Greg and Chad who let me know they cared.

For the next few months Greg would call and ask how I was doing. That meant so much to me. Today, Greg is the Battalion Chief, and Chad is Deputy Chief.

After Bob's death, I was tired and needed to rest as much as I could. Thankfully, it worked out that I did not need to go back to work so I got to stay home. It took me almost two years to get some of my energy back. I took my granddaughter, Lexi, on a cruise and spent as much time as I could with her. I traveled with friends and made my new life as a widow.

The Lord continued to lead my steps, giving me friends and family to keep loving along the way. I had been through so much grief. Losing my husband and children was extremely difficult; I will not say that it was not. Even though I had lost the most important people to me, I was not alone. God was always with me.

CHAPTER 11

Learning to Trust Jesus More Every Day

"I will put my trust in the Him."
Hebrews 2:13 (NKJV)

BOB AND I had decided to knock out a wall and put a door in so that we could have more light in the downstairs den. Well, the morning we planned to install the sliding glass door, I woke up thinking that I did not want that sliding glass door after all. I wanted a French Door instead. I decided to pray about it that morning while I was out running some errands.

Before I went home that day, I went by the store where we ordered the custom patio door and talked with the salesperson that ordered it for us. I asked him if we could exchange it for another door. He asked me if there was a problem with the door, and I told him that I had just changed my mind and wanted a French Door instead.

He told me that there would be a restocking fee of $75. I still felt confident that it was the right thing to do. When I went home to get the patio door to return, the workmen were ready to install it at my house. I called my neighbors that had a pickup and asked them if they could help me return the door to the store. They said yes and came over. We loaded the door in their pickup and headed to the store.

The man at the store told me that there would not be any restocking fee after all. I was praising God all the way home and so were my neighbors.

Now here is the rest of the story. When my husband came home from the hospital, the only way to get him into our house without having to deal with stairs was through that very door. The French Door made it much easier to get the wheelchair in than a sliding glass door. God knew all along what we were going to need, and I am glad that I listened to Him.

Many times, in my life, God has helped me to learn to trust Him more than I trust my-self. For instance, I realized that I cannot be in control of my future, only God knows what is ahead for me. I am learning each day to let Him take the lead in my life. My church family was so faithful to pray for Bob and me. Their love enveloped us every day and gave us strength to go into the next day. May God bless you for all you have done for us.

CHAPTER 12

Sharing My Story with College Students

"And God will wipe away every tear from
their eyes; there shall be no more death,
nor sorrow, nor crying. There shall be no
more pain, for the former things
have passed away."
Revelation 21:4 (NKJV)

AFTER BOB DIED, several people asked me
if I was going to write a book about what happened to my family. My first reply was that
I was not a writer. However, I could tell my
story, and thankfully, I had many opportuni-
ties to do that.

One afternoon, I was home working on
some things on the computer when the phone
rang. It was my friend, Shelley. She and her
family attended the same church that I did,

and we had been friends for a long time. After visiting a few minutes, she asked me if I would come share my story with her class at the University of Central Oklahoma. Shelley was a professor at UCO, and her class was called Psychology of Grief.

My heart was doing flip-flops. My first thought was that I could not do it, I would cry too much. I told her that it would be hard for me as it would be the first time to really talk about what had happened. I knew God had told me that my story would help someone who is going through what I went through, so I took a deep breath and answered, "Okay. I'll do it."

The first time that I shared my story with the class was during the Fall semester. The class was full of students from all professions and walks of life: EMSA employees, doctors, nurses, funeral directors, police officers, etc. In each class, there were a variety of students who would eventually have to deal with the death of someone.

Before I started to tell my story, I let them know that college students are my favorite age group, and to please forgive me if I started to cry when talking about my losses. The students were to take notes during my presentations. When I finished telling them my story, they were to give their notes to Shelley for class credit. Each time she had me come to tell my story, she would make copies of their comments and send them to me to read. I would always sit at my desk as I read their evaluations and weep.

Each student was asked to write what they saw as I spoke to them; how did it make them feel; and what did they hear me say. I want to share some of their comments with you now.

Carman wrote that she could see sadness, hurt, strength, hope, and faith in me as I spoke to the class. She felt the heartbreak in my eyes as I told about the death of my son, Craig. Carman also felt that I was still hopeful and knew that there was a light at the end of the tunnel.

Zachary wrote that he could see that I had gone through a lot of grief. He also saw the sadness that I felt when I lost my son. He explained that he had lost his best friend to suicide, and he remembered how hard that was for him. As he was listening to me tell my story, he could hear in my voice how strong I am in my faith. He liked how I included Job in my own story.

Richard wrote that he saw a woman who has so much positivity even after going through so many losses. He wrote that he heard me say, "Some days are good, and some days are bad, but do not give up. It is a choice each day to continue on." He said that he felt like he could relate to the loss of my son because he had a family friend who was like a brother to him that had committed suicide by shooting himself. This young man was bullied at school by some of his classmates, and some people were bullying him and calling him names on social media. So, he killed himself. Richard said that he had a hard time dealing with the death of his friend and tried to think about all the good memories.

Matthew wrote that he could see an older woman who is young at heart, but saw how hard it is for me to talk about what happened to my son. He said that he heard happiness and strength in my voice when talking about my amazing and supportive church family. God sent the right people to lift me up.

Madison wrote that she saw a woman who has dealt with so much pain but can still find joy in life because of her faith in Jesus. She said that she could hear my shaky voice as I talked about losing my daughter, Tamara. Madison also wrote that she could hear happiness in my voice as I talked about how God had given me a new life and a new family that has been so good to me.

Marshal wrote that he saw a strong, wise woman. He heard a woman's voice with a positive outlook in the worst possible situations. He wrote that he felt some connection with me even if it is just knowing my story. Marshal said that he had gained a better understanding of how important the community is in dealing with grief.

Oftentimes after I would tell my story, I would have students come up to me when the class was over and tell me how much my story meant to them. Many students had similar experiences to mine, dealing with suicide, death of a grandparent, and grief.

After reading the responses to my presentation and talking with individuals, it has encouraged me to continue to share my story in any way that I can. Their comments showed me that they recognized that my faith in God is what has brought me through all my losses. Without my Savior, I would have surely given up.

CHAPTER 13

Two Special Daughters from Japan

I have been blessed to have had Kayoko and Miki apart of my family. They stood by me during the toughest years of my life. I love both of you.

MY HUSBAND, BOB, and I had been working with the college students at our church for several years. Every year we would have a Christmas party at our house. We never knew how many were coming, because most of the students were from all over the world and in their culture, they just showed up. Don & JoAnne Drum, who helped us with the college ministry, always brought many students with them when they came to our house for the Christmas party.

This particular year, there was a young student from Tokyo, Japan who had the biggest smile. I could tell that she loved to laugh. Her name was Kayoko Kamata. Several times during the evening, Kayoko would come to wherever I was and start talking to me. She was sweet, and I enjoyed visiting with her. Before the evening was over, she came and asked me if my husband and I would consider letting her live with us while she was going to school at the University of Central Oklahoma. I told her that I would talk to Bob about what he thought and let her know.

Kayoko was very persistent and called

several times to find out what we were going to do. Finally, Bob told me to let her know that we would give it a try for three months. Then the three of us would sit down and talk about how it was working out. We would tell her what we thought, and she could let us know what she thought. The funny part of that story was we never had that conversation, because we loved her and really enjoyed having her live with us.

Everywhere we went, Kayoko went with us. She always went to church every Sunday morning and evening. She made friends quickly, so we usually had students at our house quite often. Having Kayoko there felt like she was a part of our family. Kayoko was very busy with her schoolwork, but quite often she would come home, and sit on our bed to chat with us about her day.

We enjoyed her sharing what was going on in her life. It drew the three of us even closer. We enjoyed the young people and loved having them in our home. Our daughter, Tamara, and her family loved Kayoko too. They always invited Kayoko to lunch or dinner whenever we were invited. My husband's sister, Jackie, also included her as part of the family. It was so nice for all of us to be together. Kayoko is a part of so many happy memories. She was a real blessing to us. As you will remember from Chapter 9, Kayoko was at home with me the morning Bob had the stroke. After we got the call from Dan who was there at Bob's office, she went with me to the hospital where EMSA had taken him. I don't know what I would have done without her.

In 2005, Kayoko was graduating with her Master's Degree from the University of Central Oklahoma. My husband and I were really going to miss her. Thankfully, Robin, the lady that worked with the international students at the University of Central Oklahoma, told us that she had another student from Japan. Her name was Miki Imura. When Robin called me and said that Miki was looking for a place to live, I told her that we could set up an appointment for Bob and me to meet and talk with her. After meeting her, we were certain that it was a good plan. We asked her if she'd like to live with us and she said, "Yes, I really would!"

When Miki moved in, it was about the time for Kayoko to be going home to Japan. We thought it would be nice to take Kayoko and Miki out to dinner so that we could all get to know Miki a little bit better. The two girls hit it off right away. I was sorry that Kayoko was going home, because I knew they would have had a good time together. We were used to Kayoko's outgoing personality, so it took time for us to get used to Miki's quiet and studious personality. Miki started to settle into living in our home, as we grew closer to each other.

We were blessed to have Miki who cared enough about us to help when we needed her. Miki was busy with her studies. If I called and needed her to help me with Bob, she was always willing especially after I had to begin working at the Wedding Chapel.

Miki became a real member of our family just like Kayoko. One day she came home from her class and told me that she had met a boy who she liked. She asked if he could come over for us to meet him. I said yes, and we met William for the first time. He seemed nice and Miki really liked him. They started dating and spending time together.

One evening I had to stay a little later at work. I called Miki and asked her if she could stay a little later with Bob and feed him before I came home. She said that she would be happy to do that for me. As soon as I got home, Miki was ready to leave. In just a few minutes she returned crying, and I asked her what happened. Between the tears, she said that she had run into our mailbox. I knew she felt bad about hitting it, so I went upstairs to hug her, and to tell her it would be okay.

After Bob passed away, I had to make funeral arrangements. Since I had no immediate family left, Miki and William, and my adopted son, Charlie Bunn, offered to go with me to make the arrangements. They took the time and stayed with me, as I made some very difficult decisions. The day before the funeral, my son-in-law, Mark, called and asked if we could place Tamara's ashes in the casket with Bob. I called the Memorial Park Cemetary and asked them about this. They said it would cost an additional $800. I went ahead and paid it and was happy that Tamara would now be with her daddy. I was thankful that Miki and William and Charlie were there with me. How good God is! He knows what your needs are better than you do.

Later on, Miki moved into her first apartment in Oklahoma City. I still stayed close with her, and we would see each other often. One day she was needing to find a couch for her apartment. So, I offered to take her out to lunch and then we could go to Mathis Brothers to browse. The first thing that caught her eye was a beautiful red loveseat. I bought it for her. She was so shocked and grateful.

I have stayed in touch with both Kayoko and Miki over the years. Kayoko lives in Japan with her husband and three children now. We correspond when we can, because she is so busy. My love for both girls is still very strong and always will be. Miki lives in Colorado. Since she lives in the United States, we are fortunate to be able to talk more often. I have traveled to Japan to see Kayoko and to Colorado to see Miki. They are both wonderful young ladies, and I am proud to be their "Oklahoma Mother". I will always be thankful for my two special daughters from Japan.

CHAPTER 14

A New Beginning for John and Judy

"And my God shall supply all
your need according to His riches
in glory by Christ Jesus."
Phillipians (4:19)
(NKJV)

ONE AFTERNOON I was working in my office, when my phone rang. I was surprised to hear a friend of mine from school on the other end, John Luton. John had been married to a very dear friend of mine, Sharon. Sharon and I were close friends in junior high school. He was calling to let me know that Sharon had passed away from cancer. I was sorry to hear the news and offered my condolences. John knew that I had lost my son and my husband, but he did not know I had also lost my daughter.

After chatting for a little while, John asked if I would like to go out for coffee sometime. I was a little bit taken back, so I told him that I was not much of a coffee drinker.

He said, "Okay, then how about ice cream?"

Reading between the lines, I told John that I was not interested in dating or having a serious relationship.

He said, "Oh no, this isn't a date. I just need to be able to talk with someone. I know you have been through the loss of your family."

John then asked about dinner. He later told me that there was a very long pause, but I eventually said, "Okay."

The evening that we went to dinner I was as nervous as a seventeen-year-old. I was concerned about what we would talk about. John picked me up and took me to Abuelo's Mexican restaurant.

Shortly after we arrived at the restaurant, I said to John, "Do you want to know why I finally said yes to going to dinner with you?"

He said, "Yes, I would."

I said, "Have you ever heard that widows love a free meal?"

We both started to laugh and that made us both more relaxed. The conversation was easy as we talked about our late spouses, caregiving, our interests, and the people we had both known in school. After the dinner at Abuelo's, he took me home. I thanked him for a very nice evening, then said good night, and went into my house.

The next morning, John called and asked if I would like to come to dinner at his house on Friday to watch the Oklahoma State University football game. He remembered that I was an Oklahoma State University fan.

I said, "Let me think about it, and I will call you back." Then I called my "adopted" daughter, Anita. I asked her what she thought I should do. She said that if I was worried about being uncomfortable, I should just take my own car, so that I could come home on my own. I told John that I would drive myself, but he did not like the idea. I gave in and let him come pick me up.

Upon getting to his house, as I was looking around, I noticed the candlelight on the table. Everything was so pretty and well kept. John had prepared a delicious dinner for us. I realized that he was a really great cook. I enjoyed our evening together. Again, I felt so comfortable talking with him. We talked every day on the phone, sometimes twice a day. I was starting to look forward to his calls.

Up to this point, not too many of my friends knew John and I were seeing each other, because I was trying to not let myself get involved too quick. John had been married to Sharon 49 years, and I had been married to Bob 47 years, which meant we both needed to be sure how our relationship should be at this time. One day, John said that it was sure a good thing we were not trying to sneak around, because he thought I must know everyone in town.

Some close friends of mine were having a Christmas party and suggested I bring John with me so they could meet him. I decided that it would be a good opportunity to introduce John to some of my closest friends.

While we were at the party, my pastor and his wife walked in. They saw us, and asked a friend of mine who that man was sitting next to Judy. She explained that it was John and that we had been seeing each other for a little while.

John heard Pastor say, "Well, is he a Christian?"

Later that evening driving home, John told me about what he had heard.

I said, "Well, that is a good question."

He said, "Well, the answer is yes."

Later, I learned that John was strong in his faith as we had started going back and forth to each other's churches.

The Wednesday night after the Christmas

party, I saw my pastor before our church service started, so I asked him, "How long have
you known me?"

He said, "Well, for quite a while now."

I said, "Do you really think that I would
ever go out with someone a second time if
they were not a believer?"

Pastor looked at me, and he said, "Well...
no I guess not."

We laughed together. I understood that
Pastor was protecting me as a widow in his
congregation and as a friend. Pastor has come
to really like and respect John.

John and I were spending a lot of time together and were starting to have some serious
discussions about life. One day, John asked
the question, "What if I were to get really
sick and you had to take care of me?"

Since we had both been in situations in
which we were the major caregiver, this was
an important discussion to have. I told him
that I was raised with the idea that when you
marry, you marry for life, through sickness
and health, 'til death do us part'. You take the
good with the bad. He agreed and said that he

felt the same way.

After we had been seeing each other for a while, we knew that God had a plan for our lives, and we had begun discussing marriage.

On May 15th, 2012, John told me that he wanted to take me to Abuelo's for dinner. When we had been there for a while, John suddenly got up from the table and got down on one knee on the floor right there in the restaurant.

He simply asked if I would marry him and be his wife for the rest of our lives.

I quickly said, "Yes! Now, please get up!!"

We were married on August 11th, 2012. Our wedding was so awesome and was attended by many of our loved ones and church family and friends. My "adopted" son, Greg Morgan, walked me down the aisle, and my other "adopted" son, Charlie Bunn, and Pastor Ron McCaslin officiated at our wedding. Both of our granddaughters sang special songs during the service. After the ceremony, we left to the music of "Stayin' Alive" by the Bee Gees. Many of the guests stood to high-five us as we went out.

At the beginning of our marriage, we were still going back and forth to each other's churches each Sunday. I had been praying and praying about where we should make our church home. The Lord made it very clear to me that I needed to follow John and make his church our home church, because that is where he needed to be. John did not feel that he could ask me to leave my church that had been so supportive of me through all my hardships of the past eight years.

We had talked early on in our relationship that we felt God was leading us into a ministry after we were married. We had been attending a Sunday school class at John's church called the FBI, Foreman's Bible Investigators. Roy Foreman was the teacher and a very close friend of John's.

A lady from the FBI class called me one day to ask if I would share my testimony at a ladies luncheon. I was excited to be asked to be the speaker. On the day of the luncheon, we had a good group from our FBI class. One of them worked for our education pastor. She told her boss about what I had talked about.

Shortly afterwards, she called me at home to let me know that her boss wanted to have a meeting with me and John in his office. I said okay and we scheduled the meeting.

After getting off the phone, I immediately went out to our driveway where John was washing the cars and told him that I had just gotten a call from the church. One of the pastors asked us to come in and talk to him.

I said, "I hope I didn't say something wrong. They may want to throw us out."

He laughed and said, "I don't think so." He reminded me that we had told the Lord that if He opened a door, we would go through it.

"This sounds like a door opening," John said.

At that meeting with the pastor, he asked if we would just tell him our stories, respectively. After listening, he explained to us that our church needed a caregiver's support group, and since we had so much experience with caregiving, we would be the perfect people to lead it. John told him that there were two things that would happen before we said yes: 1. We would pray about it, and 2. We wanted to be able to travel so it could not interfere with that. Pastor agreed to those stipulations and said that he would find people to be able to cover for us if we needed to be gone.

We went home to pray about it. We both felt like this was God's calling for us; to help others go through what we had both been through. We are both active in our church with various ministries as well as the caregivers support group. Our marriage was brought together by the Lord, and our relationship with each other is strengthened by our relationship with Jesus.

As you can see, God has been so good to us. I know that grief can change lives in many ways, but when you trust in God and lean not on your own understanding, He will be there to take care of you.

If you ever wondered if there really is a God, just ask me. I know with all my being that He loves you and me and is just waiting for you to ask Him into your heart, which you can do at any moment. God will always take you as you are. He will bless you so that you may bless others. He will hear your cry.

CHAPTER 15

Divine Encounters in My Life

"My son, if you receive my words, and treasure my commands within you, so that you incline your ear to wisdom, and apply your heart to understanding; Yes, if you cry out for discernment, and lift up your voices for understanding, if you seek her as silver, and search for her as for hidden treasures; Then you will understand the fear of the Lord and find the knowledge of God."
Proverbs 2:1-5 (NKJV)

MY HUSBAND JOHN and I were on a bus trip with our church to see Sampson in Branson, Missouri. On this bus, there were approximately 70 people, and John and I knew very few of them. The bus we rode on was called The Joy Bus. It was full of laughter and singing and praise to the Lord, along with an occasional joke from Wade our "Cruise Director."

As we rode along, we found many new friends to spend time getting to know. God showed us many Divine Encounters as we went on our journey that week. And of course, we always started our day with prayer and much thanks at the end of the day. We saw miracles all over the place. Peoples' lives were changed that week on The Joy Bus. God showed how to share His joy with others to make this world a better place. Thank you, Lord, for taking me on that trip with You!

The day that we were to see Sampson, it was raining all day. When we got to the theater, we were told to sit in the seats down in the front row, so John and I went to the front and sat next to a couple that we had never met before. We introduced ourselves to each other; our husbands were the bookends. We girls sat in the middle so that we could talk.

Their names were Jeff and Nancy McLemore. They lived in Edmond, but they both grew up in Oklahoma City in The

Village. I told her that John and I both grew up in OKC also. Next was the big question: where did you go to high school?

John and I went to Northwest Classen, and Nancy said that she and Jeff were at John Marshall. I almost fell out of my seat because my late husband had also gone to John Marshall. Nancy asked my last name when I was married the first time.

I responded, "Judy Abel, and my husband was Bob Abel."

She did know Bob but not well. Then she mentioned another boy's name that she had dated before her husband Jeff. That just happened to be one of my husband's best friends. Wow! What a divine encounter.

One of the miracles on the bus happened to me. We were coming back from seeing Sampson that evening. As we were exiting the bus, I was in front of my husband, John, going down the steps of the bus when all of a sudden, my foot slipped on the stairs and I realized that I was falling. The next thing that I saw was Wade and the bus driver holding out their arms to catch me which they did, thank

God He was there with them. You should have seen the look on my husband's face.

Sometimes God divinely connects us with people who have similar backgrounds. One morning, I was on the phone with a friend that I had not spoken to in quite some time. We were discussing how God put us together to encourage each other.

She was going through a tough time in her life as I was going through the loss of my children. A mutual friend introduced us and we very quickly became good friends even though she was a lot younger than I was. She had gone through the murder of her mother a few years ago. Her mother was her best friend, and they were very close. My friend was single, and her father traveled for a living so she and her mother ate dinner together as often as they could. She and I had a common bond: we both loved dogs, so when I would travel, she would keep my dogs for me.

She was missing her mother and I was missing my daughter. We started to go to dinner a lot and visit on the phone. It was nice because we attended the same church and knew some of the same people. I want you to know that I greatly admire this young lady because she was the one who found her mother when she was murdered. She is an amazing Christian who is very strong in her faith.

The police found the man who broke into her mother's home to rob her. This part I want to tell you is how she and her family went to see this man and told him to his face that they forgave him and Jesus loved him and died on the cross for him. Because of this the man pled guilty to spare the family of the trauma of the trial. This man is serving time in prison now. The family keeps in touch with him by sending cards and letters of encouragement. Only God can help someone to forgive like this family did.

In 2015, John and I went on a trip to Hawaii. When we landed in Kona, we met a young lady named Tina who worked at the airport. She let us know that our luggage was temporarily lost, but she assured us that she would help us find it. While we visited, she told us about her life with Jesus and how much she loved Him. She asked us if we had ever been to Kona before. We had not, so she told us about a restaurant that was close by called the Pine Tree. She said that the food was delicious and not expensive.

We decided to try the Pine Tree, and Tina was right! It was very good. As we were leaving the restaurant, I noticed a flyer on the window of a vacant building, so I walked over to read it. It was an advertisement for a church called Living Stone. I asked John if we could maybe attend that church on Sunday? He said that would be okay with him. That Sunday, we went to the church and enjoyed the service. We were both glad that we took the time to go.

The next divine encounter that I want to share is the one in which I met my sweet friend Vanessa Taylor. I had just arrived for our Bible Study Fellowship (BSF) meeting in the church sanctuary, and our leader Paula was ready to start so I went to sit down. I sat next to a beautiful young lady. I could not help noticing her coal black hair that seemed to be naturally curly. She looked like she might be of Asian descent.

When Paula finished speaking, she dismissed us to go to our small group class. I turned and said hello to the young lady. I introduced myself and she told me that her name was Vanessa Taylor. She said that she was from Vietnam and that this was her first year in BSF. We exchanged phone numbers and made plans to have lunch together and share our stories with each other.

About three weeks later, we finally had lunch together and met at a restaurant in Edmond after BSF.

As soon as she started to tell me her story, she had my undivided attention. Vanessa left her career as a physician in Vietnam to come to the United States. Her husband was a software engineer in Oklahoma since he came from Vietnam in 1975. After being in America for two years, her husband passed away from a stroke.

Now Vanessa was alone with two sons, seven and two years old, with no family to rely on and no confidence in her English proficiency. One night, she looked out of the window into the sky and wondered how and when she would recover from this situation. Vanessa had practiced Buddhism, but on this night, she said, "Jesus Christ, if you exist, would You please bring a man that can help me and my sons? If you do, I will follow you."

Four years later, Vanessa sold her house to move to California, since she had cousins that lived there. She had one-way tickets for her and her sons and had already put down a security deposit for an apartment. With ten days left to move out, her friend had called her a countless number of times daily for three days to meet an American man that was successful and good-looking. Each time, Vanessa answered that she was not interested because she wanted to focus on raising her kids, and she would only be interested if the man was Vietnamese due to the cultural barrier. Her friend said that Vanessa and this American man matched so perfectly, more than he had ever seen in any two people. This caught her attention, and Vanessa agreed to meeting this man.

When Vanessa entered the restaurant, she looked left and immediately saw the

American man, as if she had recognized him, past a crowd of people. He was well-dressed and very handsome, just as her friend had said.

When she approached him at the table, Vanessa experienced the same comfort as if she was at home. He stood up to greet her; his name was James Taylor. At this time, when Vanessa looked into his eyes, she felt that she had known him for two thousand years.

This meeting drove her to a dilemma: move to California, or stay in Oklahoma. However, James understood her confusion; with three days left to move out and go to California, James told Vanessa that if she stayed, he promised that he would help her raise her two sons, and she would not regret that decision. Vanessa stayed in Oklahoma.

Vanessa did not go to the Buddhist temple, and James also did not attend church. Every night though, James read the Bible. Vanessa remembered the time when she called on the name of Jesus Christ years before from her bedroom window. That night, she told James that she wanted to go to church. Upon hearing this, James hugged her and told Vanessa that he had been waiting for her to say this.

When I first met her, I noticed how she looked when she talked about Jesus and what He had done for her. The joy of the Lord had shined all around her. She really has blessed my life by sharing her testimony with me. We have become close friends and Sisters in Christ, and we looked forward to being in eternity together.

During a vacation to Punta Cana, Dominican Republic, John and I met many wonderful believers in Jesus. We had a marvelous time. Prior to boarding the plane for the return trip, John changed our seats for our comfort. There was a lady seated in the aisle seat who we later learned had also changed her seat. She let us in our seats and I smiled at her and said thank you, but she didn't respond. I decided to keep quiet and leave her alone.

Later I needed to go to the lady's room, so I ask her if she would please let me out. When I came back, she stood up to let me in and I said thank you and I sat down. This time she responded to me, saying you are welcome. I then realized she probably was from another country. I thought I should try again, so I turned to her and ask where she was from? She said Punta Cana, and she had family that lived there. She told me that she had been visiting her mother and a brother.

I told her we lived in Oklahoma City and most of our family lived there also. She then told me she lived in Houston with her husband and adult children. Then said she had five children, but now she only has four. I sat there not sure what to say, then she said her son committed suicide in their home. My first thought was Dear God what do I say to her? She was starting to cry and tears were coming down my face. I ask her if she believed in Divine Encounters and she shook her head to say yes. I turned so she could see my face as I told her about my son's suicide over a girl.

I ask her how long has it been since his death? She responded about four months. Then she went on to tell me that after his death she wasn't able to go back to their home, so she had been staying with one of her daughters in

Houston. The reason she went to Punta Cana was she hoped seeing her family would help her to heal. John leaned over to me to ask if they had a church family. I then ask her if her family had a church that they attended, she responded yes. Did they come to help you through this horrible time? Yes, she said they tried to do what they could by bringing food and helping to comfort as much as possible. I told her how important it was for her to hold on to Jesus and He would be right there with her family in the loss of their son. I then said how is your husband doing while you have been at your mother's house? My husband is ready for me to come home, but I am not sure I can. Right at that moment, I heard a voice say to me "Tell her that her husband and children are also grieving and they need her there with them." I told her what I had heard the voice say and I assured her she would not be alone. I shared my story and how Jesus my Savior has been with me and I know He will be with you and your family each day to help you through what is ahead.

When the plane landed in Houston, we

exchanged phone numbers and email information so we could keep in touch with each other. I knew this was a Divine Encounter from God for both of us. A few weeks later was Mother's Day. I could not stop thinking about how she was doing, so the next morning I decided to call her. The phone only rang two times before she answered and I started to tell her who I was, but before I finished, she said I know who you are, the lady on the plane and I said yes. I let her know that on Mother's Day I kept thinking about her so I ask how did yesterday go for you? She said just to let you know I took the advice about moving back home with my husband. And I had a blessed Mother's Day with my children and my grandchildren. They were happy to have me here with them. I was so glad that I had called her because she blessed me too.

Acknowledgements

THERE ARE A number of people who have been very instrumental in helping write this book. Without them I might have never been able to complete it.

The person who took the time to help me really get serious about my book was a friend from my past. Her name is Mo Anderson. Mo and I met at Metro Church soon after my family moved to Edmond.

Not long ago I was visiting with a girl-friend from church when Mo Anderson's name came up. My friend Karen asked me if I knew Mo Anderson? I answered that I did and that I had not heard from her in a long time. Karen said that Mo had written a book about her life. She was having a book signing that next week. Karen asked me if I would like to go with her. I said of course I would.

When we arrived at Mardel's, it was obvious that there was a good turnout. We went inside to find a seat before Mo started to speak. As she shared her story with her audience, everyone gave her their full attention. After Mo finished her talk, Karen and I got in line for her book signing. There were a lot of people so the line was very long, as we waited for our turn. When I walked up to Mo, she recognized me right off. We hugged and I told her I was in the process of writing my story, and if she could give me some help, I would appreciate it. She said that she would get in touch with me. I thanked her and we left.

A few weeks later I received a call from Mo's assistant asking me if I still wanted to get with Mo and talk about my book. I replied yes, I would like to do that. We set an appointment to meet at Mo's home. I was so excited I could hardly wait for the day to arrive. When Mo opened the door of her home, I felt I was speaking to the same lady I knew many years ago. Mo had not changed at all. She is so comfortable to talk with and has a down-to-earth attitude.

We sat down to talk about my book and

Mo asked me some questions about my goals for the book. My most important goal was for my Savior to be glorified throughout the book. That day with Mo I learned more about what I wanted to accomplish and was given direction on how to get there. Thank you, Mo, for giving me the help I needed to write my story.

The next person I want to thank is Julian Codding who was making cold calls as a realtor to see if we were interested in selling our house. Perhaps God had him call because He knew I needed a push to get started. Julian gave me guidance in how to organize my work and helped me many times when I would come to a standstill. He would remind me that the book would help a lot of people find hope by what I put in the book. I thank Julian for his guidance, encouragement and support.

I am not great in the use of the computer and was having difficulty with my eyesight which made it even more difficult. I knew that I needed help with the typing and organization of the book so I could complete it. I prayed to God for help in finding a solution to the problem. All of a sudden, I started thinking about a friend of mine from the church I attended before I married my husband, John. It seemed like every few days she would come to my mind. I knew she had a full-time job so was not sure she would be able to help. This friend's name was Emily Raines and I finally decided to call her.

When I asked Emily if she would be interested in working with me to finish the book, her first response was thank you Lord for answering my prayer. She was no longer working in the job I knew about and she was looking for parttime work. She wanted to be a stay-at-home mom. So, my call had answered both our prayers, and we were both very excited. Emily was a real joy to work with and her skills with the computer, English, and organization of the book have been invaluable. She has taken so much pressure and stress off me that I can only say thank you Lord for Emily.

My husband John has been a real blessing to me during the writing of this book. His encouragement has helped me when I thought that I could not keep at it like I needed to do.

He definitely stood by me as I relived my story of my losses all over again. Thank God for sending exactly who I needed just at the right time.

Last, but certainly not least, is my "adopted daughter" Anita Harris who walked through all my tragedies with me. She has a full-time job and a second job, both of which demand a lot of time and attention. Yet, when I asked her if she would be willing to edit our work, she at first hesitated. I thought she was going to tell me she did not have time but instead she asked me what if I change something in the book and you do not think I should? Could that be a problem for you? After some discussion, we agreed that our relationship is stronger than letting anything like that cause a problem between us.

Anita is very good at knowing what to say and how to say it. She knows me and knows my story since she lived through it with me. She has been an important part of my life and truly is like a daughter to me. We have been through many trials together and I thank God for her being in my life.

CPSIA information can be obtained
at www.ICGtesting.com
Printed in the USA
LVHW010000241021
701347LV00006B/29

9 781977 245229